RODEO IN REVERSE

RODEO IN REVERSE

poems

LINDSEY ALEXANDER

HUB CITY PRESS
SPARTANBURG, SC

Cover image: Billy Renkl
Cover / book design: Kate McMullen
Hub City Editor: Leslie Sainz
Author photo: Emily Brewer, Tntypes

TEXT: Arno Pro 10.5/14
DISPLAY: Uniform Condensed Medium

Library of Congress
Cataloging-in-Publication Data

Names: Alexander, Lindsey, 1988—author.
Title: Rodeo in reverse : poems / Lindsey Alexander.
Description: Spartanburg SC : Hub City Press, [2018]
Includes bibliographical references.
Identifiers: LCCN 2018005343 (print)
LCCN 2017061505 (ebook) | ISBN 9781938235412
(ebook) | ISBN 9781938235405 (pbk.)
Classification: LCC PS3601.L35396 (print)
LCC PS3601.L35396 A6 2018 (ebook)
DDC 811/.6—dc23
LC record available at https://lccn.loc.gov/2018005343

**National
Endowment
for the Arts**
arts.gov

ART WORKS.

This project is supported in part by an award
from the National Endowment for the Arts.

**HUB CITY
PRESS**

186 W. Main Street
Spartanburg, SC 29306
864.577.9349
www.hubcity.org

for Jon

CONTENTS

These are instructions for the wrangler.

—FRANK BIDART
"The Third Hour of the Night"

SAUDADE [ALL YOU PIONEERS]

Sometimes in my black dress, I move
                                        westward in wheat fields with infants
or shotguns. The canvas on the wagons drawn so taut
lightning bugs keep older pig-tailed girls like me awake at night.

                                        I've never really lived a hard life.
                                            Never rode a railcar to nowhere—

I'm an impostor from the future.

How far, how fast can my horse go? Many moons, fewer miles.

I traveled here because I thought
                               you homesteaders could help—
given your petticoats—with seasoning cast-iron skillets, with blacksmithing, with cobbling
        and bronzing
miniature, uneven pairs of shoes, their buckskin laces.

                         I know these are a spoilt girl's wishes. I may be
                                green and weak, but I'm not dumb.

Yet, have I gone back too far? The men here, all romantics—they wear
suspenders.

Oh, and how the night is clear here, the sky bright with it—

In my time, we've lost most vision of the stars.
Me? I'd love to get impressed. I text
                        LOL to everything.
I mis-belong—can't speak for us all, but—

Shh—

        All you pioneers, stand still—I press

the button to pause you
for a moment:

Your washboards caked with baking powder, a watchman stares down the wagon circle,
a woman hunched over
        the rabbit stew overcooking on the fire—

I almost press play, but instead rewind.

In an unlocked trunk, I find a brown bible, a carpenter's pencil
some man of yours whittled. I loop
        my name,
the dash, the question mark inside.

REFLECTION ON FIRST SEASON OF A MARRIAGE

Never get a husband. They never will make cheese plates without a fuss. Get a dog
with thumbs.

Sometimes when my husband does the dishes, I rampage. I rampage when
                                   for some reason the glasses look
dirtier than before a washing or I remember
                 a loneliness. I shape that loneliness into a broom. I use it to sweep
       away happiness,
a state that can often lead to complacency, and also to fly off
the broom's handle inside me.

We maybe all are holograms,
a reputable scientific journal proclaims, and I tell the husband so after dinner.

But why does this particular projection have small consciousness
                                  that wishes
to sit in a straight-backed chair and recall reciting "Friends, Romans, countrymen" in
      high school and this
                 little hologram goes to market and this little hologram hits zero
           stoplights all the way home?

Also, as a projection, I wonder at my own need

to touch. Is light drawn
to light? *Desire* light?

Why should this little light become inconsolable over the silliest—

           Oh, why is there so much of me
           in me?
               Maybe this is easy

science: Each hologram an imagining light thought to construct,
     in which one furry projection drinks from the toilet, one projection sprouts leaves
that fall annually and never improves
                         at leaf-retention, and my husband—

an invisible who may not exist in the kitchen behind me
if it weren't for his singing.

SLEEPLESS IN INDIANA, I CONTEMPLATE THE AGE-OLD ARTS

Dog that won't stop barking and all I can think:
I don't know anything about stars—

not what they're called or how they form, but how

we turn stars into stickers to surprise
our children and assure them *You are better
than normal children.*

On boat decks, sailors cry out *Orion!*
                      and they see a man,
but they've only drawn stick-figure self-portraits
of fire and longing.

             I tried to sketch
my face one night with stronger brow lines,
higher cheekbones, but it was all nose, scaly
water moccasin: a viper me.

I paid someone who drew me in
red with big hair, gaunter—
the way he drew me made me

see how lonely he thought I was. I rolled
that portrait with wax paper and a rubber band,

            look at it during the Lenten season.

That same spring or summer on the back of a boat, I caught a sunfish, baited him
with gum. I didn't like unhooking him—

tore his lip. Astrologists
shape stars into fish, take cracks at

decoding futures. Palm-reading hocus-pocus:

on my hand—which is starboard,

                               port, and which is solar flare?

I could use that hand to throw a tomahawk
from this bed and hit neither boat nor star

from way down here,
so far from water.

SPRING STORM

My sister was young and bicycling before
she died last night
in my dream. *Dreams aren't subtle,*
she'd said to prove a point.
Dreams don't fuck around.

People in my dreams age backward—
my sister's breasts still smaller than mine,
her legs still
longer, but I stay
my awake-age, always.

The wreck petrified
the witnesses—a woman and her child,
who both looked like me, except
they wouldn't talk,
wouldn't show me

the body. She had pedaled
into the road, been hit,
which the newspaper
detailed in its color pointillism
photos—my sister in chalk

outline, my sister's bicycle
a commemorative art display in the future.
An older man had found her, had called
the too-late ambulance—
I could feel her missing

from me, and her missing felt like my face
waterlogged

to violet, so I woke.
In a thunderstorm,
in our double-bed years

before, she once hushed
me, *Don't worry,*
but oh how
she kicked in her sleep.

WHAT IF THROUGH A WINDOW, THOSE ONES?

What if a person's whole
life were looking quietly
out a window?

*That's not a new idea, but whether it's a sad story depends
upon the view I reckon.*

What if outside the windows were the ancestors
of your lover?
Outside—a slow conveyer belt,

a parade, a mugshot lineup, a reverse death
march of the ones who made the one you love.

Can covetousness break glass?
Seep through the casement like a draft or
a bad odor?
How to thank—

Do not think about the thoughts of the long-gone
people on the other side

of the window. They cannot see
you and probably would not wish
to if they could.

But I thought our forebears look down on—

This is not heaven. This is an exercise.
With a window.

This is an exercise on looking.

Ah.

What do you see?

Aprons.

Good. What is in the pockets of the aprons?

Coins.
I can't make out the amounts or dates, but they are coins
of varying circumference. No bills.
The waistbands—some of them have
rickrack or frills.
Now I understand
my fortune. Thank you.

You cannot see inside the pockets.

But you—

You know nothing of the ones who made the one
you love. You do not know
their motivations or worries or hairdos except

their worried eyes and picture-day hairdos.
You do not know the wear
of the tread on their bootsoles or whether they wore slippers to bed.

This is not a metaphor.
This is an exercise, an exercise
on looking, which always means imagining,

which means tying together right and wrong and half-right and half-wrong
like a bouquet garni and tossing it thoughtlessly
into the pot, steeping until having
                              flavored everything.

ELEGY AT TWENTY-THREE

for Brian

Jon's brother's best friend died. She was twenty and likeable.

I made a hamboat and brought over some Bud Light.

Later we all went out to karaoke. I was sadder when my dog died,
but I knew more what to do then, too.

I always wore my seatbelt until this happened,
when I stopped.

What does all that even mean?

In the paper a while back, I learned how at the zoo in my hometown
an elephant's fall resulted in cracked ribs and its killing—

We went to karaoke. But they would only show the lyrics in Japanese,
so really we were just dancing with our breath

of tequila and French fries. Pop song,
pop song, pop song:

whatever we wanted, we thought we took it.

Eliza's hair was shorter than yours until you cut it then it was longer and she was dead.

SELF-PORTRAIT WITH GOLDEN AMMO

Easter's over, meaning it's time again to resurrect
my vices. Did that boulder Sisyphus was lugging ever
roll anywhere? Me, I prefer a scrappy Prometheus thieving
fire when spring swells tired: every dawn another liver.
In Savannah, Sherman marched but did not burn;
and in that respect we differ because you see,
I want to burn it all. First vice: quick to ire, second:
pride, the most maligned. The antidote? Last season's leftover ashes
which I'd spread on my forehead to level it, to square it,
to remind me of strange sin until I can't abide it.
In heaven, I'll still wait to hear ammo made of gold drop, drop
into the chamber of a gun that I redeem, buy, or steal, to say,
And I know how to use it. What is it, that story about the barrel,
its one apple spoiled? Seeds filled with cyanide to begin with,
mixed up in my core. A woman sees a tornado coming,
throws herself into a ditch. Once in the ditch, she sees
a wildcat in there, too. Now that's a parable.

GOOD ME ATTEMPTS TO NEUTRALIZE, RESCUE, OR OTHERWISE STIFLE BAD ME

Oh ne'er-do-well, be quiet now.
Pick up the splinters from your over-
the-falls barrel—I'll save each chip

for kindling later. I've seen the feats
you've death-defied to death. If you must
get a tattoo, get a tattoo

of a grid; on it we are each a dot,
parabola between us. We're never
more than rise-over-run away

from that downward slope
you reel us over. Have one more hit
and go to bed with it. I'll unpack

your suitcase while you're sleeping.
I'll fold your clothes to boot. I'll leave
a note:

Bad Me,

Do not press the Do-Not-Press-
This-Button Button. Brush your hair.
If the doorbell rings, don't answer as Lindsey.

Yours,
Good Me

I wonder if you wonder if it's bad

that there's the two of us in here:
you with your Bowie knife, me
only darning needle–equipped.

I do. Think it's bad, I mean.

HONEST ABE GETS MAD JEALOUS OF THE PRETTY, SUCCESSFUL GIRL FROM MY HIGH SCHOOL

You are tall, but I
am Lincoln. I tower over you
                with my addresses and bolo tie, the worn-out sound
of my backwoods accent, and my mythic rail-splitting
backstory.   Sure, you look fine in flowing
             maxi-dresses and I'm a depressive,
but they're never going to give up one minted cent
for you. Here. Have two of mine, my two cents:

Beauty is overrated. In fact, it can act as Satan's limb.
        It sends emancipation and other five-dollar words blazing
                through my temple.
                                But you wouldn't understand.
                Neither would you know how hard it is to drive in Illinois
where all the license plates repeat
                        a face like mine
        as they tailgate me and then pass and slow down—I'm cutting myself off
        constantly in the land of me. Revel in your silver
                spoon, your anonymity, your white-stripped teeth,
                        and moleless neck—

                        Perhaps I should rise above these petty grievances
        and from my own ugliness to my own height, but *whether I shall
        ever be better, I cannot tell.*

                I awfully forbode I shall not.

URGENT MATTER

John Lennon never was
my favorite Beatle.

Take one look
at George Harrison—you'll know why. Those teeth, yeah, those cheekbones.

Who is an album cover to you?

Your perfect ring of hair, bright, a halo—have you never been
as old as me? Things are wrong empirically until

an exception is made. I always except myself.

For instance: there's nothing holy in virgin hair. Mine's been bleached a dozen times.
You're welcome.

Is marriage a mistake only young fools make? No,
old fools, too.

Better yet: two houses

connected by breezeway. Oscillate between *It's nice
to see you* and *It's nice to be seen.* A second look

at John
with Yoko, so fashionable with their sleep-ins,
refrigerator-closets for all their furs.

SCRAP OF MAIL FOUND NEAR TRACKS OF OVERLAND ROUTE

It's hard to be a pioneer, I know, to split
the wood, to shoot and skin the bear,
greet the trail with cheer each morning. Difficult

to fix the spokes of wheels, to master

the particular tilt of any coonskin cap.
Typhoid and other fevers razing
his every log-cabin fantasy. Fine.

But can he even see me under this bonnet?

My apron strings drag near to the floor
with sadness, no bow, just knot,
tying each to the other. Before him,

my own dairy farm dream of

cows and butter. He sold my one
cow to ford a river, to be
closer—

to what?

We've seen the geysers, territory, territory,
and marveled at the bad lands' beauty.
No, not charmless—

campfires at night, his thick wrists

tense as he gripped the reins, how he'd dip
his kerchief in a tin cup of water,
press it to his neck....

But all the dirt.

I am pilgrim-
worn and plenty tired.
I am trying to be generous.

THIS BONE SHALL DRY UP AND HOPE SHALL BE LOST

If sister threatens sister with kitchen shears,
      slicing each crusty blade an inch from her throat, let us rejoice
and be glad in it. For hers is the kingdom

of the world. She who needs salvation
      seeks it. Or she doesn't, and drags sister
by the hair down the staircase.

If an idea of grave sin should invade sister's mind,
      she kicks holes in the door. Ply them with spackle
before Mother and Father get home

and your family shall be passed over. In the belly
      of a whale, don't be the one spit back into the sea.
Be the one who devours the whale

from the inside out and surfs to shore
      on a giant, buoyant bone. Strike the bone
on the ground. Open, then close the sea,

      and let sister, still swimming, drown.

SAUDADE [UNSPILL THE SALT]

Think of my hair
in the light:
how it's tangled and tosses

itself over my eyes
awful preciously. I planned it
that way. It's hard

leaving, and slowly,
too—the horse moving like
the old kind

that gives pony rides:
it knows its route. Salt
moving forward, salt

looking back. It was always like
a prism hanging in the kitchen
window with us,

refraction
and surprise. But somehow
it just got unhung.

How to unring?—
To unspill
the salt?—How

to unwarp
what we've been
woven into?

GUILTY AND RECKLESS, I TRY TO MEET THE TORNADO HEAD ON

Bicycle: hold my cards in your spokes for this dumb spin.

Indiana reminds me
        that right before the tornado,
          the world—

        it's all golden and fresh like a warm loaf of bread, like honey drizzled
          over every last thing, the cracks

    in the sidewalks sticky with honey and the dogs would bend at once to lick it,
the ants stuck, the birds' beaks stuck
        closed with sweetness.

Later, the dogs are full and I don't eat,
          and I don't eat,
       and then
         I try to think of something geometric and pleasing like
          a suspended staircase:

    each of its steps held up by mathematics, tiny excuses and explanations
    science asks us to believe in.

            Me: an ancient wheel,

       a Fibonacci sequence:
    ammonite-me, hardened impression of the girl who used to be:

my slouch an apology rendered
        and re-drawn by nature—the *sorry, sorry*
       stuck to my surface
       like a slug.

       The tornado never
    touches down.

           Some consolation.

LOVE FROM PARIS

Eating a sandwich and reading Toni Morrison at a park in Le Marais,
I think of you but do not really wish you were here.

On the postcard I send you: a description that isn't quite precise
about children pushing toy boats out into a pool of water
with long sticks.
How composed French children are. Meanwhile, a man
walks up and down the Seine without his pants on,
pulls shorts out of his shirt pocket, puts them on, and keeps walking.
I write *I wish you were here* in French.

I picture you, too large for our car, huddled in:
you won't turn the radio on.
You talk about the man who bought his father-in-law's tree-cutting business, found he
    was afraid of heights—
the fields and fast food signs racing behind to reveal
more fields, more signs.

I can't help but think of the leather work glove I saw in the snow
with no footprints around it.

I can't help but feel you
would appreciate that—that inkling we both like something
about being together roughly
as much as leaving alone.

THROUGH GREENHOUSE GLASS

After the Civil War, war photographers' best customers
were gardeners.

Photos of dead soldiers unmarketable—
their negatives now greenhouse glass
panes. What plants grew

under light distorted by curled soldiers' faces? Under its steady stream,
which of those stills seared away first—
bodies in lines or piles, tents or ruins? Not the trees, with their million

sorrows of bitter crop.
What other implement than terror to bend us
toward some greater will? Against

those panes, knock
knock. *What?* I said, Knock knock.
Who's there? I don't know.

I Don't Know Who?

I don't remember—
Oh, right.

THE WAITING ROOM

An absence of clocks in the rooms where we sit
in overstuffed or plastic-armed chairs
making our most important decisions.

The only shuffling of papers, the paper I shuffle myself.

Sometimes bordered wallpaper spices things up.
In a relative's house: the Amish suicide pact—two faceless
pilgrims back to back, slumped—a pattern repeat. Impossible
to paint over. Difficult to remove.
Who could have chosen it?
Other times a vase
of silk or plastic fauna. Love's austere
and lonely offices, maybe they hold a single bouquet
in muted tones at the reception desk.

I fasten my top button.
No—
unfasten it.

Less
surreal.
Even plainer.
Less sensual, more living
room. The phones blurt; the cars move through the picture
window like a reel, like the carousel of image behind
a still car on a movie set. But less romantic and with far less
money.

IN WINTER I WATCH

after Laura Ingalls Wilder's The Long Winter

the seasonal annoyances shed
their bare–tree limb omens, me reading
them like washed-out tea leaves. I don't know how

to crystal ball the what's next of things, so instead I read
the density of snowfall, count the birds at the feeder, wonder at how
they and the squirrels stay warm and forget myself

and the crow and
what it might mean, the wind scraping

at my cheeks. I think of a young woman training to be a schoolteacher on a homestead
                                                     caught

in a blizzard, her small world

a letter she'd been drawn into
erasing itself before
her—red smudge of hotel, wooden smudge of grocer, straight-edge of steeple—gone, going, gone
   first.

She formed a slash mark against the weather
of it:
     blank *or*
blank.   This   /   walking

home from a one-room schoolhouse—
the *or*
     moving about, not understanding
the motion of her bargain—
her eyelids, still bruise-colored
like a baby's, bleeding at the cut of the terror of wind.

WATCHING SONNY AND CHER REUNITE ON LATE NIGHT WITH DAVID LETTERMAN WHILE CONSOLING CHAZ BONO, 1987

ZOOM IN: An album cover
taken on their old bed, where
        you, Chaz, may have become more
        than thought, the fusion of two
sets of lavender pajamas.
Letterman coaxes them. He wants

        "Got You, Babe." Cher says no. But
        your dad wants to give it a try—
I could tell.
As the band unwinds chords

        like a broken clock, the cue cards drop;
        Sonny's eyes squint and his thin
lips quiver. She sings over
and over him, much
        taller, much louder. She pretends
        he's forgotten

the words. He knew but couldn't
form them.
        Hey, don't worry, Chaz,
        they'll pull this off, they'll make it

just in time for an encore chorus,
holding each other's
        too-much hair, laughing.
        My parents went through
this part, too; most people's do.
They've called the lawyers

        and they've had a few drinks
        and hurts too many, but this doesn't end

there. I can sense
by the roots of your yellowing

  hair: every negative leads to one
  conclusion—watch his eyes, look
how she shakes her dress. When you're away
at a friend's Malibu Dreamhouse party,
  she'll pat the white chenille coverlet
  on the brass bed, your father's gold

chains dangling, and the bed
will get unmade. They'll unmake

  and unmake it.

THE DREAM AND A SHAME

I was an observer: my own student
and my best teacher
in the forest working the lyrics together.
There were bees in his beard,
in a good way.

She cupped his chin: this
was platonic and also the source
of some honey. He fed her
two lines he had kept inside his soul
for years. I woke to write them and could

only remember *alone*.
He left and she
grabbed a banjo from a tree—
completed the song and bettered
it, besides. Something like "The Passionate Shepherd"

but blue, which the Impressionists
knew to put a touch of in every shadow.
CUT TO: the sprung-open backs of a dozen watches.
Time was
busted; still

I didn't fix the hands of clocks I could have moved.
The bells and cuckoo birds,
the dancing German ladies
with their aprons and their steins
shilly-shallied willy-nilly

throughout the day. And anyway,
I've learned naught if I haven't learned not
to tell anyone when he or she

has appeared in a dream—
he or she never takes it the right way.

It does all sound unseemly, I admit—especially the horse, which I'll get to.

Though I do want to ask—
I'm working on a theory—
if the song or the honey skips
a generation, the same as twins
or a quick temper?

Before the dream I was thinking of the horse
who bit the cowboy so you could see straight
through to his skull.
The horse that won't be broken isn't a romantic
story—it's a shame and ends

with the horse hurting
a human then being put down.
Damned if I don't worry that the horse is a mirror,
like the trainer says. Damned if I'm too afraid to push myself
out even so far as my own dream.

I only have two tools:
attention and inattention.

The rest—
just for show.

But credit where it's due:
that banjo in the tree was a nice touch, subconscious,
a real lucky break.

ON THE KING BRIDGE IN FRANKFORT, KENTUCKY

A tugboat tugs across the water—a coal load for Christmas again.
That boat's only strategy: slog through, slog through.

On one end: the men at the White Lite Diner, staring down their burgers—

On the other, the library with clouds painted on the ceiling
to look like clouds outside.

The children who don't hide in the library
bicycle and bathe in an idyllic, warm TV glow.

Growing up for me
was fine, except on a bike
I was a pansy.

Idyllic childhood kids are braver.
Some pass over the bridge in song now,
their tires playing the grates like a steel harmonica—

I piddle
with my zipper. I fidget.
It's unattractive.

         No minute
thoughtless—each thought acute, *acute*
meaning tight squeeze, meaning
                  serious.

The tugboat blips and bleats.

A nickel pushed over the rail, can't hear it drop or sink—to think, the night's never
quiet enough.

Oh, Lindsey, you've complexed this bridge:
                  just a thing to cross
the water. But, looking down, I can see the water, too.

SPAGHETTI WESTERN IN WHICH BAD ME CHALLENGES GOOD ME TO A DUEL

Let's settle this.
Take ten paces.
On the count of three,

we draw. The loser,
well—no more,
bygone, adiosed.

My last request?

When the credits run,
list me
as *Lindsey*,

not
the Good
or Bad One.

WHERE I THINK I MIGHT BELONG

A diorama: Here are the stars of foil, here
the tiny workbench, there the cloud, the grass,
the river moving fast, and there is Tiny Me
set here just plain: knob-head, yellow yarn me.

We are dogs on leashes, her and me. We're dots
on grids—A4 when she leans on the toothpick fence
at the shoebox edge, D3 when I'm searching shelves for glue
that will keep her house from pulling apart; my hand

pulling through Tiny Me's hair. In the box, there's no
early morning or birds going south—there's no song
at all except what I sing myself. A stone
in the river or a cat swimming circles over

my blue cellophane body of water. Close the lid
on my box, and Tiny Me swims like that.
She doesn't like taking her clothes off
in front of me. When we dream, we dream

about how scythes spin and lassoes in old Westerns.
A helicopter's blades spin, but also its wheels and also
gauges inside of it. Unlike the birds that aren't
in the box, I don't know much about flight.

But if I lift the box, it's like Tiny Me is flying.
Words have a sweet spot in the box's corner,
memorizable index card wonders: *subdue, substantiate,
subsume*—the field in the shoebox and the field

with gray sky pressing it flatter can fulfill these
words, we think. My dog made of corks and my papier-mâché
hill, and my dog lying beside the radiator—they
are all plotted by some sort of coordinates, too.

SUNDAYS FROM 11 TO NOON EXIST FOREVER INTO ETERNITY

Sunday's echo chorus, *A-men, Ah-men,*
Aw man, pews again. The hymnals ripple
open, pages thick and edged
blue with the off-key voices' raftering, the plates
passing like a hat around a honkytonk late at night,
but in the morning, here. Civil War quarter notes
shouting our triumph in bloody God's battle
to end something and shield ourselves with the white Wonder
Bread cut into squares for wafers. Clearly it's not the body, can't be the body,
wholly—
        We drink the juice together, unfermented holy.
Barbara's cancer is in remission, but Tammy waits for her test results. The Hoskins
mourn the death of their uncle, the services
precede the youth pitch-in on Thursday; please be sure to donate canned goods, please be
seated.

Some kid pours the font-water fresh every week,
and most weeks he pours it down the drain
unused. But those others—
how babies' skin sprinkled softens—
show even the hardest tap water can act as Water of God, worthy
of sacrament for our heads and our feet that are equal
in eternity. This week
we lay hands on the man we voted to accept
as a member. No communion,
being only the second Sunday of the month,
but we share Styrofoam cups of lemonade
in the gym-converted Fellowship
Hall. The younger ones sip theirs through coffee stirrers.
We make the decisions and God abides,
or He does the making and we the abiding by.

AFTER NATURE, EVERY LAST THING

I've put out or hung over
the bannister to

            air out.

Memories made yesterday are today's stench:
marijuana, sweat, bug spray.

On Sunday, I didn't go to church. Still, I prayed

for a scenic view—an ocean or mountain, a single paddleboat on a lake
full of a couple.

What I got was dust
caking my feet, and I couldn't

help but think I'm more

like Jesus now
with these dirty feet than ever prior.

A newly gained appreciation for foot-washing as sacrament. How disgusting and intimate.
Mary Magdalene. What a broad. Picture

a new incarnation

of myself, tripping, in body paint. Prouder
of and shaking what

the good Lord gave me.
But at the end of the concert, I'm, as you guessed, the same person. Just more cognizant

of dissonance, a musical way of saying distance from

what feels right.
Transformation isn't as easy as biting

a wafer, drinking from a thimble, kneeling.
The Eucharist, brush across the arm, the set

of notes struck in triumphant succession—only for a measure.

The work of it's more to do with belief. The miracle's just a part of the waiting. Like,
get this: After coming down from space, astronauts must lie in bed for weeks.

STILL LIFE WITH BREAD

In art books, the cornucopia
drawn beside the skull, a pear fallen
out, a stein with foam running down all placed
on a wooden table. They show perspective
but also class and skill, my sister or a museum curator
sort of taught me.

Like a favorite boot placed beneath the mantel,
this moment of dough
arranged, a hearthstone,
for viewing. The beauty of
                        things, my favorite
of leather and fur, brass finish and cognac-dye, or,
I'll cop to it: bedazzled, gluten-injected,
arbitrary.

Domestic life is such a bore, Hollywood
and professors of some schools say.

Yet above the refrigerator the bread dough rises.

To know the self intimately who washes
the face, frames flowers picked
from neighbors' yards, poses in her comfort
pose on the lawn chair. She is me; me equals
                                  mundane.

The still life of me wouldn't include me yet I would still

recognize it
             by brushstroke, by content and composition—
how the light hits it, its practiced nonchalance,

the coyote pelt.
Even the difficult clementine
shrugs off compliments, though impossible to render

                accurately bald and bright and plain—
how many thousand circles and arcs overlapping, never quite enclosing—
in oil.

            But back to the bread—I must
look away for a while, always, sometimes
leave it for sleep or
to walk the dog—precision
in baking, yadda yadda, the flour scraped
over the copper measuring cup's lip, anxiety beating
its steady digital alert—*It's time!* My husband can shout
He is risen!
like from the Bible, only it's funny
                because

it's not about a Saviour.
A savior might look leftward (as one must
from the right hand of the Father) and note
a certain stoutheartedness here in Indiana, in our bad jokes
and repetition, each morning breaking miracles of
more then more *more.*

I SAID I SAW AN OSTRICH BURY ITS HEAD IN THE SAND AT THE ZOO, BUT

ostriches don't actually bury their heads in the sand.
They do, to be fair, hunker down, hiding their heads to act like a bush—either way,
                    a bird that has a hard time
                              with flight and fear. It's an old wives' tale I've transposed
                    in place of some realer memory—

true,

        but I've said I remember seeing it that way at a petting zoo.

            Though maybe, the ostrich—like me—hopes
                                        to find a backbone in the modesty
                                        of bending or burrowing.

            In appearing smaller, one might unlock the ancient codex

                                        by not-flying, not-fitting
                                        but by focusing on shrinking to

                    a moment, hiding—
                              fusing to what's hidden—

                    by burying one's head
                              with such purpose.

COLOR THEORY AND OTHER WHEELS

So much effort expended
on time. The magic trick I can do: turn busted
glass on the road into diamonds under sun. An optimist's game.

It's October, and here I am again—
blue. Primary—primal?—
and cool. Lapis lazuli,

Lepidoptera. In Florida,
thousands of butterflies
pressed into wall—one sort of garden.

The jewels collected and never worn.
The furniture in the historic home, a sign:
Do not sit here.

The past in the present—I'm not allowed
to touch. But it's on display,
and like a bobbin underneath, tension maladjusted,

it pushes through,
catches or knots up any delicate design.
Better to hand stitch, to clutch,

than to rip seams, unwind, but all
the time I have already
let pass. Something or other about what's behind glass—

the ache of being
pulled both forward and back, except
inanimately. I look and overlay

my reflection onto a terra cotta parrot and think
of a real flapping parrot
at the zoo—how I could see

the red flight, my face, around it, and through.

THE CONFUSION OF LIGHT

Let's circle back, one bird suggests at the end of winter.
The flock flocks.

Round like a hatbox, perfect
and cylindrical: their swoop of leave-taking, their return.

I watch them
take off. Give or take six months, I watch them land.

What a landing, I say.
I've been standing at the same window, waiting

all season. Animal ritual. Birds have their dignity, humans
our small trespasses. Me: I'm a spy. Forgive us
our debts—I learned to say *debtors*

at church, not like the line they say in the movies.
Sin as something monetary.
Guilt as a thing owed until

it isn't. A penny for my penance.
I remind myself not to talk

to birds, or else
I'll end up like that *tuppence-a-bag* woman, a loon.

Besides, birds know what
of guilt, what of holding in
a sorry, a sorrow, the confusion of light?

At night a star pulls me up like an alien beam toward
a more thoughtful, appreciative existence.
But just before,

the small flame of a match burning me right
to the quick.

DISPATCH

I suspected there might be fireworks in heaven.
It's like shooting them off in the backyard, except
nobody here can lose a hand. We shoot them off
clouds, let their embers fall into American national
parks, spark forest fires. *Think before you burn,*
we whisper before we kiss them goodbye.

There are those fingerless gloves with mittentops here,
and no moths to eat holes through your favorite sweaters.
Everyone with their Missoni Slankets and designer shoes—
we are all comfortable, attractive, and flame-retardant
in what must be the Omega, where cigarettes
are dipped in honey. When we flick the butts,

the ashes taste like miracles to the silly living below.
Although sleep isn't a necessity, there are cots for naps
or consensual copulation, because after all,
we're supposed to be having a good time.
Sometimes, we look down on Texas,
pretend we're watching syndicated *Dallas.*

I knew for sure everybody else would beat Larry Hagman here.
Sure enough, we all did. When rockets get launched
into space, we laugh at how far they never go, like those fish
that jump out of manmade ponds and people call them flying.
We still take bets on basketball brackets, and everyone wins; the lottery, too.
Everything's money in heaven.

ONE-POINT PERSPECTIVE

Mountains full of wild
horses—someone make them
bow down.

All things must wear
away, eventually,
someone said, I'm sure.

So why not rather now
than later? Flatten
out to prairies

and plains. I'll run across
them then, my arches aching
for I won't know when

to stop. I'll race each horse,
until they are big
and I am small against

that dusk horizon: my aim
to reach the vanishing
point long before the horses do.

THE NEGATION IS THE POINT

The Socrates I like really doesn't know anything:
a gadfly can't be smug.

If S. were a lady, she would say
sorry many times a day. Instead of revolting, would she maybe
admire the miniature

woodland creatures in the museum, carved
from sucked and spat-out peach pits? The glitter-glue round
the turkey's neck, the hummingbird's wings, its back
hollow. As a young artist, the whittler,
she would wonder if he were considered

"an odd fellow"

because
near-nothing and -being met
at his pocket knife's blade.
Or didn't he realize?

But would S. ask? My guess is no, for probably discomfort in others
made her uncomfortable, though she was comfortable
in her own discomfort.

Is S.'s silence less important than S.'s question?

I consider this over buttered toast. I press my finger against the table
to collect each crumb.

I enjoy passing the time with Mrs. Bovary and eating toast, drinking gin and lemonade
in the sun, watching a dog stretch or run, the idea
of gardening.

I'm unlikely to admit to knowing not a single thing.
I'm still working on not sharing

      every thought I think or wonder

in upward inflection.

What makes a lady interesting?
What she chooses
to disclose?

CONSTITUTIONAL

When you are gone, you are gone,
unless you are Patty Hearst. Then, Tania, you are only play-acting.

But those TV crime-moms, what were they
thinking? Is it human to want to kill your own child?

I clean under my nails.
Possibly. But the one who drives her kids right into a lake—I bet she doesn't regret it.

Expert after expert: Post-partum depression.
The standard old-guy narrator despises her. Enticing,

but a little disheartening. I congratulate myself for this sensitive feeling. I nom my Egg
    McMuffin
and close my copy of *Lolita*: page 123. Humbert's got nothing

on the real thing—that woman who cut off her ex's penis?
Woah. This month I've also discovered Butter Puffcorn to be addictive.

Watch this:
In a flick of the wrist, I produce a new channel:

Snapped!
crime-wives who off their husbands. I watch a half-dozen. What a snack!

What a rush! A scheme foiled—What a narc! What a plunge!
Programming I can get behind.

For another paper-towel, I get up.
I go for my walk: I check the locks, double-locks. I pet the dogs.

They bark at noon. The mail comes at three.
Hiding myself, but I manage.

THE RADIO IS FULL

of people singing in-love
love songs. It's spring and the sun has shown up
after flaking on evening plans for a season,
but the band isn't holding grudges. Neither
are the fans—we're all happy for the lead singer's return.
Welcome back! I'll buy the T-shirt for the memories.
All the leaves on everything coming to fruition
like palm readers have predicted for years:
the little plants photosynthesizing merrily,
the big plants photosynthesizing above. The wind
moving away
papers, sheet music; just enough of a wind
to blow off work and to convince me to freewheel.
The cars in the parking lots aren't driving like maniacs, nor are their drivers.
They're just forgetful and blissed out.
The shandys fill the aisles—I buy some for
the thrill; Easter grass is on sale. The grocers on their breaks
laugh on the patios not in the cynical way
of winter grocers.
Kinder.
The Vitamin D—
oh, who cares about the science? What about dancing?
I'm not even kidding:
A yellow butterfly Axl Rosed past me on my way out the door
into the world that is
in love with itself.
A major narcissist.
But an attractive one—
a mistake (today today today I feel it's one) worth making twice.

IN THIS CASE

*"Thus the soul is not in the body, but the body in the soul, and the soul is
the entire network of relationships and processes which make up your
environment, and apart from which you are nothing."*

—ALAN WATTS

All year, I gathered
the felled light.

I felled the gathering light all year.

I'm not sure which—I wrote which
down on a scrap somewhere.

Perhaps my husband buried it with the coffee grounds in *la poubelle* (a fancy French sort
of trash can).
I will squint and punish him just for the thought of him thinking of it.

Very well.
All the better.

If I stand still as any just-shy-of-living thing, a pinecone sunk
into snowmelt, for instance,
                        re-frozen—
the neighbor cat may return to lick the salt at my imitation
leather bootheels.

And the cat, the boots, the salt, the light, the *and* may be
abandoned into the fear of *la poubelle*, may be mixed in with the mail.

The contrivance inherent in my waiting—

All these part of a small bright prism in the Lindsey event.

The little days come and go, and go and go
does the event of Lindsey, a tea party
for only so long as the light decides to fell
                        in the sightline of her.

GOOD ME'S SAUDADE OF BAD ME

Bad Me remembers before she was born.
She claims being not-yet-born

                                    is an enclosure to itself,
like a hidden hook

                 and eye
on an expensive dress,

     and mostly,
                I think,
     I believe her:

She peered onto the crowns
of the heads of the already-born,

                          and she readied herself.

        Though I was not-yet-born too, I don't recollect this process at all—
        A small group of monks may have prayed me where I now am.

Were we still the same then—no bad me, no good
me, just the one?

The past with her hand cupped around us, as one would care for, as one would protect,
   rodent—

Those earlier memories:
                       where Bad Me's badness likely derives itself.

       What is it
               like,
    having a Bad Me?

I'll tell you:

We're melted
to munition, the bullets gunslingers shoot into passing
railcars out West.

Bad Me snug, at ease
inside the barrel
of our home-gun—

How can she call me Good One
when it's both of us

in the chamber, attending
the trigger's command?

*

She's dangerous.

She's useful.

I miss her.

ART HEIST AS THOUGH A HEART

A dozen doors hinged on the same frame—
like at the hardware store except
each plastered with master sketches of ballerinas
and similar ingénues. I'm passing
the time passing my prime staring at
men's visions of other women, afraid to ask
the docents the history of classics, of symbolism.

In any case, I've known so many Europas,
the white bulls of Titian, Rubens,
whoever dragging them downstage to their dooms.
Rapturous or rapacious—I wager
the experts disagree.

I'm the blurry friend at the edge, waving
my hanky in distress. Sputters the heart
inside me, me swinging the doors, dreaming up
lunch, knocking the doors into
one another—collider of lovers. I used to write as if
I had no heart, as though the word *heart*
were cilantro: for some, flavorful garnish;
for me, hard to swallow. Genetic.

In my former life—the one I have imagined into
a butter mold of a person
I'd like to have been—
I went to Catholic school in Britain right before the mid-century.
From time to time the nuns
made us wash out our mouths with soap.
We weren't martyrs—my legion
of knee-socks and midi-skirts. We necked
and took the Lord's name in vain. *But*

the blitzes! But the rations!
The nuns heard our objections
but insisted we behave.

Back to reality, the missing art:
I stare at the empty,
gold-gilded frames, big as me, as four
of me. Despite the Rembrandt label, I espy *Alice and Wonderland*–style
through the looking glass
a Van Gogh,
not a painting but the famous Dutchman.
Still two full ears, a sort of failure
but of a different sort. He stands before
a bleached-out bucolic scene:

wheat field, gray sky, I can almost see
the cows mooing without moving their mouths in the distance.

The man foregrounded,
wearing barely any clothes;
yes, in tatters, there he is, the legend filled
with light but next-to-no
color.

I touch his palm and the whole
picture wavers, ripples. Like Christ
he calls but I cannot follow.

LANDSCAPE MYOPIA

The panoramic view—I am a part
of each scene too, but I can't stand back far
enough to get it

down or take it in. Closer, easier, a snowy egret tips its hat
to me, proverbially. My epiphany?
My periphery and blind spot—the fly-away blur, the not-quite end.

BUT WHAT ABOUT THE MOON

*I can see the reflection of the window in your eyes but you are not looking
at the window,* he said, divining the morning
weather, the light diffused in fog.

That is correct.

But what about the moon?
(which was still visible; it was early in the day.)

Just then a tuning fork sounded—with it,
the retired fireman next door had unintentionally cast a spell
but neither could place it and so, after some discussion, they turned over to sleep in
the sun coming through the window, no longer visible in the one spouse's eyes,
and didn't awake for epochs, until she was well past her childbearing years
and his glasses prescription no longer sufficed.

The woman, rising, cursing her bruisey arms, realized she had wanted
not a husband, but a twin, but a husband
would do in a pinch.

SUNSET ABSENT HUSBAND

A rock's memory is forbidden to us.
A rock's memory is forbidden to us.
The striations, the convergent boundaries—where Earth pieces have crashed,
are visible; geologists can read them.
And yet, rock's memory is forbidden to us.

A leaf's brevity is unknowable to us.
A leaf's brevity is unknowable to us
though I watch my husband grow older raking new leaves each year.

I am glad for this husband, who knows the pink in the sunset
the intensity of a fruit I have not eaten
does not appear everywhere.

I am glad he knows and hope I will
never forget,
                    no matter whether remembering may hurt.

(I will forget; I have for hours or weeks at a time.)

I am glad to have and hope
to be glad to have had—
                    though I suspect that joy is rounder, like the old rocks, far-off,
                    and harder won.

    Here and there, bare and inscrutable, a single wildflower between two.

For now I am glad for now because now
I remember what I know my husband knows,
am seeing what he has seen and remarked on on several occasions.

BUT WHAT OF THE WIFE

of the Buddha? Did she, like the horse,
die of heartbreak, sunset watercoloring, leaving

much to be desired behind
her crumpling silhouette?

No.

Did she, like a flower at the end of season,
die of shame?

No.

Did her friends gift themselves piteous looks,
take turns leaving

warm food beside her unlocked door?

Probably.

She was a good wife. She bore a son and combed her hair;

she had the servants rearrange the chairs and practiced
the art of splendid seductive tear creation,
which amateurs know as crying.

For the horse, enlightenment proved fatal.
For the woman, I imagine enlightenment chronic,
an affirmation of an unspoken truth itself a treasure, like a hand-embroidered espadrille
or a sclera-white pet duck,

a perfect parting gift.

Upon his return, she made eyes but refused to sit for weeks at a time in protest.

Yet because of wisdom or love or desperation or vengeance
she asked for his hand in perpetuity,

which is (I believe) Buddhist legalese for other lives, if we are to believe the stories,
which we are to believe.

SPIRITUALISM

In the evening, I don
                    full-mourning,

the next evening, half-mourning. I own a dozen
shawls, dyed to shades of winter sky, and the Ouija board
                                        does its work.

Everyone who's lost someone knows the meaning
of butterflies, the widow said.

I didn't, a red one now
stuck between window and screen.
                              If I wad its wings like a paper ball, toss them in my
                                      mouth like a grape?
Clamp the teeth shut.

A revelation I trace with my hand:

The Good Death is a one that sticks.
Essentially *Beauty, Truth, Truth, Beauty.*

His face (not Keats') gaunt and glowing, a light bulb above my head,
the electricity of which
                        I cannot figure.

In heaven I hope for heaven's sake
we each lose every memory.

But the usual doubts.

SAUDADE [BOTTLE ROCKET]

Kiddo, halt this bottle rocket. Cork its mouth
so the ideas don't lose their flavor while no one's listening.

Some men say the soul's a circle,
                              and it's possible, sure, that souls could work
like Venn Diagrams' overlapping or like
horoscope charts.
              (Coincidence sometimes feels so fateful,
so fatal.) But mine's more a line extending out farther,
farther from me—
              an arrowhead at both ends, shooting.

That's how growing feels—like the man accused
of witchcraft, strapped to the pressing rack, *more weight, more weight*—
                              a stretch toward death.

Recall the lion that has a man position his head inside its mouth, slowly,
the beast that won't bite down,
                              the will Aesop's lion exerts
                              in not eating the mouse.

    Or consider the insistent modesty of a brown dwarf star:
                                                  one that fails
              to ignite, only detectable by its gravitational pull.

For some time, I replaced my bedtime prayers
with the steady counting of worries.
But things have changed.
                    When now I lay me down to sleep,
I request that if I'm good, I'll come back
as a horseshoe,
              feeling the ground for the horse
because the horse ought not to feel it.

HOMESTEAD, SURE

But then there's the beauty of the rodeo:

the buck and nod,
                    that arch and stretch
        against gravity.

        A bronco's no square peg,
and neither am I.

                Pegs or no, we both flex
                        our more resistant muscles—

                strong-legged, strong-willed.

To learn might
            is the ticket.

The power of my unrelenting?

                    When I expose
                            exactly
            how pure, how—
                    if stubborn enough—
                        entire I can be—

ACKNOWLEDGEMENTS

Thank you to Sean Hill for making all the difference to me in selecting this manuscript.

Thanks to the editors of the following publications, where some of these poems originally appeared, sometimes in earlier forms: *Arts & Letters*; *Colorado Review*; *Crazyhorse*; *cream city review*; *Devil's Lake*; *DIAGRAM*; *Fifth Wednesday Journal*; *Forklift, Ohio*; *Green Mountains Review*; *Grist*; *Grist Online*; *Hayden's Ferry Review*; *The Lumberyard*; *The Mackinac*; *The Mondegreen*; *The Southern Review*; *Third Coast*; and *Waxwing*. "Saudade [Bottle Rocket]" and "Where I Think I Might Belong" also appear in *New Poetry from the Midwest 2014*. "The Dream and a Shame"; "Homestead, Sure"; "Sleepless in Indiana, I Contemplate the Age-Old Arts"; and "Reflection on First Season of a Marriage" also appear on Poets.org.

Thanks to the National Endowment for the Humanities for necessary time to delve into another writer's work and revise my own. Thanks to Bruce Gentry and Bob Donahoo for organizing the 2014 NEH Summer Institute "Reconsidering Flannery O'Connor" and to my fellow O'Connor scholars, who also happen to be many of my favorite people.

Thank you to the Purdue University English department, my classmates, and my former poetry students.

To the women at Hub City—thanks for being as fantastic as I imagined you to be. To Meg Reid for being the voice of reason; Kate McMullen for making the process—even typesetting—seem seamless, which I realize is no small feat; and Leslie Sainz, for being a friend, for being indispensable, and for her attention to these poems.

Thanks to those who have supported me as a friend and as an artist, often as both and beyond measure, especially: Greg Allendorf, Andrea Alumbaugh, Sara Amato, Ali Arant, Rhonda Armstrong, Analise Brown, Jeanette Booher, Larry Buchanan, Katie Condon, Brian Hines, Julie Henson, Sara Henson, Allison Hutchcraft, Jessica Jacobs, Rebecca McKanna, Monica Miller, Rosalie Moffett, Piyush Nandanwar, Jeremy Reed, Kelsey Ronan, Kirsten Schofield, Ashley Smith, Jacob Sunderlin, Corey Van Landingham, Meagan Van Hess, Natalie van Hoose, Rachel Watson, and Jen Woods.

Thank you to my teachers, particularly: William P. Bradford II, Maureen Morehead, Sue Collesano, Don Belton, Alyce Miller, Maurice Manning, Kathy Smith, Porter Shreve, Wendy Flory, Mary Leader, and Don Platt. To Marianne Boruch, who has been a dear friend to these poems and a great help to me, for all the help and orange wedges.

To Jessie the dog and Dolly the dog.

To my family, my grandparents, and my parents, Gil and Lisa Alexander—with more love than I can say, and especially to my sister, Cassandra.

Finally, to Jon—if I could write how much you mean to me, I would've put it in a poem.

NOTES

1. *Saudade* is a Portuguese word that was explained to me as an intense longing, a yearning for, a kind of nostalgia stronger and more complicated than the kind we have words for in English. I looked it up a few years later to find it also is akin to a homesickness for something or someone that never quite existed, mixed with real and imagined memories, that residual feeling.

2. *Satan's limb* is what it's rumored Mary Todd's step-mother called her.

3. The italicized lines in "Honest Abe Gets Mad Jealous of the Pretty, Successful Girl from My High School" are direct quotes from Abraham Lincoln's letter to his law partner, John Stuart. From the letter: "Dear Stuart: ... I am now the most miserable man living. If what I feel were equally distributed to the whole human family, there would not be one cheerful face on the earth. Whether I shall ever be better I cannot tell; I awfully forbode I shall not. To remain as I am is impossible; I must die or be better, it appears to me. . . . I fear I shall be unable to attend any business here, and a change of scene might help me. If I could be myself, I would rather remain at home with Judge Logan. I can write no more." It is dated January 23, 1841. Full text available at House Divided: The Civil War Research Engine at Dickinson College.

5. The title of "This Bone Shall Dry Up and Hope Shall Be Lost" references Ezekiel 37:11.

4. The Fibonacci Sequence is a geometric series discovered by none other than Fibonacci. It is a pattern of numbers that regularly occurs in nature, such as the numbers of petals on a flower. It also explains the shapes of spirals in nature, like the scales on a pinecone or the curvature of ammonite, which is an extinct species that's left behind many shell-like fossils.

5. I owe my sense of bargaining to Alice Munro. In her story "Post and Beam" she writes, "It was a long time ago when this happened. In North Vancouver, when they lived in the post-and-beam house. When she was twenty-four years old and new to bargaining."

6. The horse stories and the horse trainer in "The Dream and a Shame" come from *Buck*, a documentary about Buck Brannaman. "Your horse is a mirror to your soul," he says, "and sometimes you may not like what you see. Sometimes you will."

7. Tom Petty said, "The waiting is the hardest part." He was mostly right.

8. An art heist took place at the Isabella Stewart Gardner Museum in 1990. Among the bandits' thefts were works by Rembrandt, Degas, Vermeer, and Manet. One of the ways the museum marks the loss is a large frame—empty—labeled Rembrandt.

The New Southern Voices Book Prize was established in 2013 and is a biennial prize awarded to an emerging Southern poet who has published at most one previous collection of poetry. It is awarded for a book-length collection of poems written originally in English.

HUB CITY PRESS

HUB CITY PRESS is a non-profit independent press in Spartanburg, SC that publishes well-crafted, high-quality works by new and established authors, with an emphasis on the Southern experience. We are committed to high-caliber novels, short stories, poetry, plays, memoir, and works emphasizing regional culture and history. We are particularly interested in books with a strong sense of place.

Hub City Press is an imprint of the non-profit Hub City Writers Project, founded in 1995 to foster a sense of community through the literary arts. Our metaphor of organization purposely looks backward to the nineteenth century when Spartanburg was known as the "hub city," a place where railroads converged and departed.

RECENT HUB CITY PRESS POETRY

Magic City Gospel • Ashley M. Jones

Wedding Pulls • J.K. Daniels

Punch • Ray McManus

Pantry • Lilah Hegnauer

Voodoo For the Other Woman • Angela Kelly

Waking • Ron Rash

Home Is Where • Kwame Dawes, editor

Checking Out • Tim Peeler

Arno Pro

10.5/14